Creativity in Business

A Practical Guide for Creative Thinking
Revised Edition

Carol Kinsey Goman, Ph.D.

A Crisp Fifty-Minute™ Series Book

This Fifty-Minute™ book is designed to be "read with a pencil." It is an excellent workbook for self-study as well as classroom learning. All material is copyright-protected and cannot be duplicated without permission from the publisher. *Therefore, be sure to order a copy for every training participant through our Web site, www.axzopress.com.*

Creativity in Business

A Practical Guide for Creative Thinking

Revised Edition

Carol Kinsey Goman, Ph.D.

CREDITS:
VP, Product Development: **Charlie Blum**
Editor: **Karla Maree**
Copy Editor: **Charlotte Bosarge**
Production Editor: **Genevieve McDermott**
Production Artists: **Nicole Phillips and Betty Hopkins**
Artwork: **Ralph Mapson**

Trademarks
Crisp Fifty-Minute Series is a trademark of Axzo Press.

Some of the product names and company names used in this book have been used for identification purposes only and may be trademarks or registered trademarks of their respective manufacturers and sellers.

Disclaimer
We reserve the right to revise this publication and make changes from time to time in its content without notice.

ISBN 10: 1-56052-533-9
ISBN 13: 978-1-56052-533-2
Library of Congress Catalog Card Number 98-74645
Printed in the United States of America
9 10 11 12 09 08

Learning Objectives For:

CREATIVITY IN BUSINESS

The objectives for *Creativity in Business, Revised Edition,* are listed below. They have been developed to guide the user to the core issues covered in this book.

THE OBJECTIVES OF THIS BOOK ARE TO HELP THE USER:

1) Identify characteristics of creative people

2) Explore techniques for encouraging creativity

3) Understand the ways creativity can be destroyed

ASSESSING PROGRESS

A Crisp Series **assessment** is available for this book. The 25-item, multiple-choice and true/false questionnaire allows the reader to evaluate his or her comprehension of the subject matter.

To download the assessment and answer key, go to www.axzopress.com and search on the book title.

Assessments should not be used in any employee selection process.

About the Author

Author, keynote speaker, seminar leader, and consultant, Carol Kinsey Goman, Ph.D. is an internationally recognized expert on managing organizational change, developing creative potential in individuals and teams, and conducting business globally. She has been cited as an authority in media such as Industry Week, Investors Business Daily, CNN, and the NBC Nightly News with Tom Brokaw. Her client organizations include Bank of America, ARCO, AT&T, Motorola, Prudential Insurance, Pacific Gas & Electric, the International Association of Business Communicators, the Young Presidents' Organization, and the American Society of Association Executives.

For information on her speeches and seminars, contact Carol Kinsey Goman at Kinsey Consulting Services, P.O. Box 8255, Berkeley, California 94707. (510-526-1727). You can also reach Carol by email at cgoman@ckg.com or visit her website at http://www.CKG.com.

To the Reader

According to a recent survey, when senior managers were asked to state the most important and valued traits in workers, they said creative problem solving and new ideas. In business, creativity can help you launch major projects or untangle minor snafus. It provides a fresh insight and new perspective on even the most routine elements of your job. Best of all, it enables you to view problem solving as a creative opportunity!

Sound like magic? While it can work wonders for you, creativity isn't some mystical force or extraordinary talent possessed by the lucky few. Rather, creativity is an ability everyone (to one degree or another) has. Even better, it is also a skill you can develop more fully.

This book was designed to help you uncover more of your innate creative potential and then develop techniques that will allow you to "tune in" to your creativity at will.

Each section of *Creativity in Business* leads to a better understanding of how to become a better idea-generator and innovative problem solver.

Learning to use more of your creativity will allow you to rekindle that spark of excitement about work, to be more confident in your ability to confront situations with fresh ideas and more innovative solutions, and to take advantage of the creative input of others.

Get set for a wonderful journey as you explore your personal creative talent. And good luck as you develop this ability into results-producing actions!

Carol Kinsey Goman, Ph.D.

Carol Kinsey Goman, Ph.D.

Contents

Section 4   Group Creativity

Section 5   Innovation and Practical Solutions

SECTION 1

Getting Started

> " *The human mind, once stretched, never goes back to its original dimension.* "
>
> –Oliver Wendell Holmes

2

What Is Creativity?

Years ago in a newspaper column of Ripley's "Believe It or Not," the following item appeared: A plain iron bar is worth $5.00. If you take that iron bar and forge horseshoes from it, the value increases to $10.50. If it is made into needles, the value rises to $3,285.00. And if you make watch springs from it, it then is worth $250,000.00. Ergo, the difference between $5.00 and $250,000.00 is creativity.

Definitions

> *Creativity*: Bringing into existence an idea that is new to you.

> *Innovation*: The practical application of creative ideas.

> *Creative Thinking*: An innate talent that you were born with and a set of skills that can be learned, developed, and utilized in daily problem solving.

> *Creative People*: Those people who do not block their innate creativity and who focus their ability in various aspects of life.

Everyone Is Creative

There was a time when the dominant opinion held that just a few departments of the organization housed creative people—perhaps marketing, communications, or product development. In the old framework, only top executives had the intelligence and insight to solve problems and develop new concepts. Such limitation not only placed a great burden on the "creative few" to come up with all the answers, it put restrictions on the contributions of workers who were most knowledgeable about the situation. Most importantly, this widely held belief about selective creativity was flat-out wrong!

Creativity is needed at every level and in every function of an organization and everyone in an organization is capable of being creative. A factory peopled by skilled laborers can encourage and benefit from creativity as much as the most high-powered think tank.

Case In Point 1

It was a factory employee of Period Furniture, a manufacturing company in Henderson, Kentucky, who devised a solution to the problem of dropped screws on the plant floor. Screws were a safety concern and often flattened the tires of the plant's trucks. The employee suggested that magnets be installed on the bottoms of all company vehicles driving through the plant. The magnets picked up the screws, thus eliminating the problem.

Case In Point 2

And not all products are created in R&D labs, either. Liquid Paper® was invented by Bette Nesmith Graham. In the 1950s, she was working as a secretary. She corrected typing errors with a bottle of white tempera paint and a small brush. She noticed, however, that the tempera brushed off the paper too easily leaving the error visible. She began experimenting in her kitchen and discovered that nail polish provided a more permanent solution. In 1979, Ms. Graham sold her company for $47.5 million.

YOU ALREADY ARE CREATIVE

In what areas of life do you display your creativity? (A hobby, work, relationships, public speaking, art, music, crafts, and so on.)

_____

_____

_____

Where have your creative ideas been put to practical use? (Party you hosted, report or project you designed, unique approach to a presentation, and so on.)

_____

_____

_____

What was the most creative thing you did as a child?

_____

_____

_____

Where in your life would you like to apply more creativity?

_____

_____

_____

What people (living or dead) are or were creative in ways that impressed you?

_____

_____

Your I.Q. (Intelligence Quotient)
Is Not Your C.Q. (Creativity Quotient)

The late Dr. Richard Feynman was one of the world's leading theoretical physicists. After being awarded the Nobel Prize in Sweden, he flew to his old hometown and stopped at his old high school. While he was there he looked up his grades. They were not as good as he had remembered, so he asked to see his I.Q. score. It was 124—only slightly above average. He was delighted. "Winning a Nobel Prize is no big deal," he reportedly told his wife, "but winning it with an I.Q. of 124 is really something!"

What's your C.Q.? Take the quick quiz on the next page.

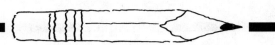

EXERCISE: HOW HIGH IS YOUR C.Q.?
(CREATIVITY QUOTIENT)

Using a scale of 1 to 3, take the following quiz to check your Creativity Quotient.

Score: 0 = Never   1 = Once in a while   2 = Sometimes   3 = Always

_____ 1.   Are you curious? Are you interested in other people's opinions, other departments' problems, or customer feedback?

_____ 2.   Are you a "creative opportunist"? Do you find opportunities for solving problems, creating wants, filling needs?

_____ 3.   Are you a strategist? Do you spend time redefining your goals, revising plans to reach them or creatively using organizational changes to correct your own course?

_____ 4.   Are you a challenger? Do you examine assumptions, biases, or preconceived beliefs for loopholes and opportunities?

_____ 5.   Are you a trend spotter? Do you actively monitor change in your field such as technology, government regulations, or new management strategies to spot opportunities early?

_____ 6.   Are you a connector or adaptor? Do you watch for concepts you can borrow from one field to apply to another?

_____ 7.   Are you a risk taker? Are you willing to develop and experiment with ideas of your own?

_____ 8.   How's your intuition? Do you rely on your hunches?

_____ 9.   Are you a simplifier? Can you reduce complex decisions to a few simple questions by seeing the "big picture"?

_____ 10. Are you an "idea seller"? Can you promote and gather support for your ideas?

_____ 11. Are you a visionary? Do you think farther ahead than most of your colleagues? Do you think long term? Do you share your vision with others?

(CONTINUED)

(CONTINUED)

_____ 12. Are you resourceful? Do you dig out research and information to support your ideas?

_____ 13. Are you supportive of the creative ideas from your peers and subordinates? Do you welcome "better ideas" from others?

_____ 14. Are you an innovative networker? Do you have colleagues with whom you share creative ideas for feedback and support?

_____ 15. Do you attend lectures or read books about the "cutting edge" in your field? Are you fascinated by the future?

_____ 16. Do you believe you are creative? Do you have faith in your good ideas?

_____ SCORE

Check your score using the scale below.

SCORE YOUR C.Q.

41–48   Reveals that you have a very high creativity quotient. You will find creative ways to put the techniques in this book to use!

33–40   Shows you're mentally ready to explore more of your creativity and should do very well using the techniques and exercises presented.

25–32   Indicates that you have yet to discover your true creative capacity. By practicing some of the ideas in this book you should be greatly encouraged by the positive results.

Below 25   Suggests that you may be surprised by the increase in your creativity after using this book. You don't know yet how creative you can be!

How High Is Your C.Q.? (Creativity Quotient) was adapted from <u>Motivating at Work</u> by Twyla Dell, a Crisp Series book.

2

Creativity Blocks and Blockbusters

> "The way to accelerate your success is to double your failure rate."
>
> –Tom Watson Sr., founder of IBM

You Were Born to Be Creative

In the late 1940s, a group of psychologists were discussing the lack of creativity in most adults. They speculated that by age 45, there was only a tiny percentage of the population who could think creatively. To prove that assumption, they designed a creativity test and gave it to a group of 45-year-olds. Less than 5% were creative as determined by their test scores.

They continued testing by reducing the age of the subjects. They tested at ages 40, 35, 30, 25, and 20 years old. The 5% creativity figure stayed basically the same for all these groups. Finally, at 17 years old, the percentage of creative individuals rose to 10%. At age 5, it skyrocketed to over 90%!

The conclusion? Almost everyone is highly creative at age 5!

QUICK CHECK:
BENEFITS FROM ENHANCING YOUR CREATIVITY

Check (✓) each statement that you believe to be true for you.

Increasing my creativity at work can:

❑ **Help me make the best use of my talents, aptitudes, and abilities.**

❑ **Enhance the enjoyment of my job.**

❑ **Cause me to have more self confidence.**

❑ **Cause me to be a more valuable employee.**

❑ **Enhance my opinion of myself as a proficient problem solver.**

❑ **Ultimately increase my income.**

❑ **Cause me to become more self motivated.**

❑ **Help me to feel more innovative and "intrapreneurial."**

❑ **Give me a greater sense of control and mastery over my job.**

If you checked even one box, it should motivate you to learn techniques presented in this book to increase your C.Q. (creativity quotient).

Blocks and Blockbusters to Creativity

Blocks to Creativity

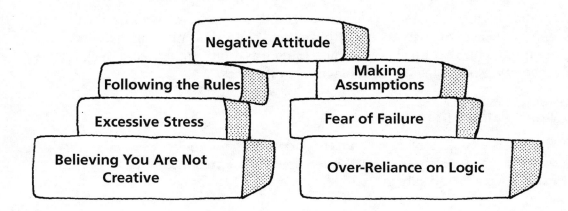

Creativity Blockbusters

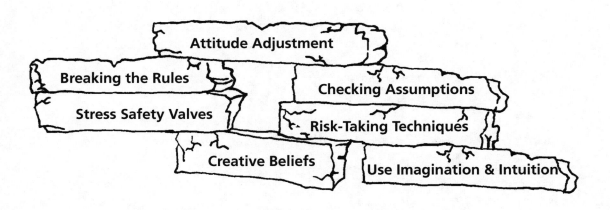

Discover what blocks your creativity—then develop a blockbusting strategy!

Block #1

Negative Attitude

In Chinese, the ideogram for crisis combines two characters; one is the symbol for danger, the other for opportunity. Pessimists, by nature, will turn their attention to the negative aspects of a problem and expend creative energy worrying about possible detrimental outcomes. Optimists, on the other hand, will liberate creativity by focusing on the inherent opportunities.

Don't Believe the Experts

Negativity is ingrained in our society and our organizations. The following quotes are humorous and, at the same time, potent reminders that even the experts have historically greeted new ideas with negativity.

"That's an amazing invention, but who would ever want to use one of them?"

> –U.S. President Rutherford B. Hayes, after participating in a trial telephone conversation between Washington and Philadelphia in 1876.

"The horse is here to stay, but the automobile is only a novelty—a fad."

> –President of Michigan Savings Bank, 1903, advising Henry Ford's lawyer not to invest in the Ford Motor Company. (Disregarding the advice, he invested $5,000 in stock, which he sold several years later for $12.5 million.)

"Who the hell wants to hear actors talk?"

> –Harry Warner, Warner Brothers, 1927.

"I think there is a world market for about five computers."

> –Thomas J. Watson Sr., Chairman of IBM, 1943.

"Television won't be able to hold onto any market it captures after the first six months. People will soon get tired of staring into a box every night."

> –Darryl F. Zanuck, head of 20th Century Fox, 1946.

"There is no reason for any individual to have a computer in their home."

> –Ken Olson, President, Digital Equipment, 1977.

For more about the importance of attitude, see <u>*Attitude: Your Most Priceless Possession,*</u> *by Elwood N. Chapman and Wil McKnight, a Crisp Series book.*

BLOCKBUSTER #1

ATTITUDE ADJUSTMENT SCALE

Read each statement and circle the number that reflects your current attitude. If you circle a 10, you are saying your attitude could not be better in this area; if you circle a 1, you are saying it could not be worse. Be honest.

		HIGH (+)									**LOW** (−)
1.	If I were to guess, my feeling is that my boss would currently rate my attitude as a:	10	9	8	7	6	5	4	3	2	1
2.	Given the same chance, my co-workers and family would rate my attitude as a:	10	9	8	7	6	5	4	3	2	1
3.	Realistically, I would rate my current attitude as a:	10	9	8	7	6	5	4	3	2	1
4.	If there was a meter that could gauge my sense of humor, I'd rate a:	10	9	8	7	6	5	4	3	2	1
5.	My recent disposition—the patience and sensitivity I show to others—deserves a rating of:	10	9	8	7	6	5	4	3	2	1
6.	My attitude about my own ideas and creativity is:	10	9	8	7	6	5	4	3	2	1
7.	My attitude toward other people's creative ideas is a:	10	9	8	7	6	5	4	3	2	1
8.	Lately, my ability to generate lots of possible solutions has been a:	10	9	8	7	6	5	4	3	2	1
9.	I would rate my enthusiasm toward my job during the past few weeks as a:	10	9	8	7	6	5	4	3	2	1
10.	I would rate my enthusiasm about my life in general to be a:	10	9	8	7	6	5	4	3	2	1

SCORE _____

A score of 90 or above is a signal that your attitude is "in tune" and no adjustments seem necessary; 70 to 89 indicates that minor adjustments may help; 50 to 69 suggests a major adjustment is needed; below 49, a complete overhaul may be required.

This scale was adapted from <u>Attitude: Your Most Priceless Possession,</u> by Elwood N. Chapman and Wil McKnight, a Crisp Series book.

Block #2

Fear of Failure

Fear of failure is one of the greatest inhibitors of natural creativity, and yet every successful innovator has failed often. Tom Peters, the renowned management guru, declares that the prescription for dramatically increased innovation is dramatically increased rates of failure. Those who embrace failure as a product of creativity definitely have the advantage!

BLOCKBUSTER #2

RISK-TAKING TECHNIQUES

1. What is one creative risk you are currently considering?

_____

2. Why is it important for you to take the risk?

_____

_____

3. If you took this risk and failed, what is the worst possible outcome?

_____

_____

4. If this approach failed, what are your other options?

_____

_____

5. How do you plan to deal with this failure?

_____

_____

CASE STUDY: FEAR OF FAILURE

As a woman in her thirties, Vicky was being groomed by her father to take control of the family business. Vicky told her best friend: "This is such a wonderful opportunity. I have so many new ideas about how to improve the business. I only hope that I don't let him down!" The friend replied: "What would happen if you tried your best and still failed to meet your father's expectations? What if he didn't like your ideas?"

Startled, she replied, "Why, I'd feel perfectly awful!" Then her friend asked: "What would you do after you felt awful?"

Vicky wound verbally through an entire sequence of reactions. She fantasized leaving the area, changing her name, and finally joked about putting herself "up for adoption." At last she smiled and said, "I guess I'd have to find a way to survive."

Based on her response, do you think Vicky is a creative person?

❏ **YES**   ❏ **NO**

Block #3

Excessive Stress

Psychologically, an over-stressed person finds it increasingly difficult to maintain objectivity and has trouble perceiving alternatives. This is often accompanied by a great sense of pressure based on having feelings such as not enough time, too many demands, or being trapped. The arousal of such distressful emotions will usually result in poor creative thinking and reduced decision-making abilities.

BLOCKBUSTER #3

STRESS SAFETY VALVES

Place a check (✓) in the appropriate column. Rate yourself candidly.

Do very well 1	Average 2	Need to improve 3	I am succeeding at:
_____	_____	_____	1. Taking responsibility for my own stress (not blaming others).
_____	_____	_____	2. Knowing my optimum level of stress (where I do my best).
_____	_____	_____	3. Balancing work and play.
_____	_____	_____	4. Loafing more (learning when it's appropriate to do nothing).
_____	_____	_____	5. Getting enough sleep.
_____	_____	_____	6. Refusing to take on more than I can handle.
_____	_____	_____	7. Exercising regularly.
_____	_____	_____	8. Setting realistic goals.
_____	_____	_____	9. Practicing relaxation exercises.
_____	_____	_____	10. Taking pleasure in the here and now.
_____	_____	_____	11. Valuing family and friends.

Do very well 1	Average 2	Need to improve 3	
_____	_____	_____	12. Managing my time and setting priorities.
_____	_____	_____	13. Taking time for recreation and hobbies.
_____	_____	_____	14. Avoiding too much caffeine.
_____	_____	_____	15. Emphasizing good nutrition in my diet.
_____	_____	_____	16. Avoiding alcohol or other chemicals to deal with pressure.
_____	_____	_____	17. Avoiding emotional "overload" (taking on problems of others when I am under stress).
_____	_____	_____	18. Giving and accepting positive "strokes."
_____	_____	_____	19. Talking out troubles and getting professional help if needed.
_____	_____	_____	20. Selecting emotional "investments" more carefully.
_____	_____	_____	21. Taking breaks at work when needed.
		_____	**SCORE**

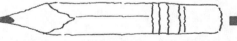

SCORE YOURSELF

Between 50 and 63, there are several areas you need to develop to better release your stress. It might be a good idea to discuss some of your answers with a counselor or close friend.

Between 21 and 51, you have discovered a variety of ways to deal effectively with stress. Make a note of those items you checked "Need to Improve" and work on strategies to help you move to the "Average" box.

20 or lower–Congratulations. You have found some excellent ways to deal with frustrations and the complexities of life.

This exercise was adapted from Stress Management, by Merrill F. Raber, M.S.W., Ph.D. and George Dyck, M.D., a Crisp Series book.

DEEP RELAXATION

Creativity is not just a mental game. The relationships between thinking and feelings, mind and body, are critical to unleashing creativity. Tension constricts the flow of ideas through the mind as it constricts the flow of blood through the muscles of the body. The simple act of physical relaxation frees the body of muscular tension and frees the mind to be open to new ideas.

Here is a technique for getting into a relaxed state. Soothing, low, rhythmic background music helps to create a relaxing mood.

STEP 1   Get comfortable; loosen any tight clothing.

STEP 2   Focus on your breathing—deep and even, slow and rhythmic.

STEP 3   Close your eyes and imagine yourself in a pleasant, tranquil setting—by a lake or in a beautiful meadow filled with flowers. Visualize the scene. Imagine what it would be like to experience this place. See it. Smell it. Taste it. Feel it. Listen to it.

STEP 4   Become aware of each part of your body, beginning with your forehead, then chin, neck, torso, arms, and legs. Picture your body as a balloon with air slowly escaping from it until it is depleted and limp.

STEP 5   Let go of conscious effort. Picture your mind as an expansive blue sky. When individual thoughts enter, picture them as birds emerging from a distance, flying over your head, and disappearing again into distance.

STEP 6   Slowly, silently, count from ten to one and let yourself relax deeper with every number.

STEP 7   Remain in this state for at least 10 minutes. As you begin to refocus your thoughts, you should experience a sense of calm, a sharpened ability to focus attention and, perhaps, a deeper sense of appreciation for the creative force within you.

CASE STUDY: BUT WE'VE ALWAYS DONE IT THIS WAY

At one time, the New York Fire Department's rulebook stated that fire crews were to place a ladder against the front of a burning building before doing anything else.

There was a fire. The brigade arrived. The lieutenant of the brigade noted the fire was raging in the back of the building and rather than waste time putting the ladder against the front, as the rules required, he ordered the crew around to the back to put out the spreading blaze. The fire was put out quickly, minimizing the danger and potentially saving lives.

But one of the Fire Department's inspectors was in the area. His job was to see that things were done according to the rules. He noted the absence of the ladder against the front of the building and began disciplinary action. The union got involved and a court cased ensued.

In court, the defense lawyer for the lieutenant asked why the rule was in the book. No one, not even the chief of the brigade, knew the answer. Then the lawyer brought in an historian who testified that nearly a century earlier, in New York City, there were no full-time, paid fire fighters. All the brigades were voluntary and the insurance companies would pay only one brigade—the first one at the scene of the fire. How did the insurance company know which one was first? The first to arrive would put its ladder against the front of the building!

For all those years since the end of the volunteer fire brigade, no one had questioned the policy manual. No one had ever asked: Why are we following this rule!

 Tip: *Here is a key question to determine the current validity of established rules and regulations: We may have "always done it that way," but if we hadn't, would we start doing it that way now?*

Block #4

Following the Rules

While some rules are obviously necessary (for example, we should all be happy that there is a consensus agreement about stopping at red lights), others thwart innovation because they encourage a mentally lazy acceptance of the status quo. Many inventions and innovations in a particular industry have been brought about by people outside of that industry. Why? Because the people who make the creative breakthroughs are not hampered by knowing all the rules and limitations.

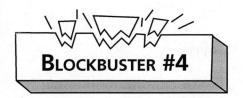

BLOCKBUSTER #4

BREAKING THE RULES

It is not always a bad idea to break certain rules—especially as they pertain to your daily routine. Check (✔) the following "rule breakers" that you would like to try and write the date you'll put it in practice.

	RULE BREAKER	DATE
❏	Take a different route to work in the morning.	_____
❏	Eat lunch at a new restaurant.	_____
❏	Eat a different kind of food at lunch.	_____
❏	Skip lunch and go roller skating or jogging.	_____
❏	Come to work in the morning and pretend it is your first day there. Write your reactions.	_____
❏	Come to work in the morning and pretend you are a customer or a competitor. Then write up your reactions.	_____
❏	Sign up for an activity you have never tried before.	_____
❏	Invite someone you don't know to have lunch or a conversation with you.	_____
❏	Read a book on a topic about which you know nothing.	_____
❏	Take a weekend to go somewhere you have never been.	_____
❏	Ask for advice from someone whose opinion you have never sought (spouse, child, janitor, client, stranger).	_____

What other rules would you like to break?

_____   _____

_____   _____

_____

What is preventing you from breaking them?

_____

_____

Block #5

Making Assumptions

A recent story told about how the Research and Development manager of a large high-tech firm found supplies and test equipment missing from a laboratory store, so he ordered the installation of a security system. Several months passed without any further losses.

While preparing a routine report for the president of the firm, the manager noticed that progress on a couple of key projects had slowed down. Concerned, he decided to investigate. He discovered that several technical research engineers had stopped working on the projects at home on weekends because they could no longer get supplies and test equipment. The R & D manager had erroneously assumed dishonest employees caused the missing supplies. He had, therefore, "solved" the wrong problem. Making ironclad assumptions often inhibits creative thinking about other possibilities.

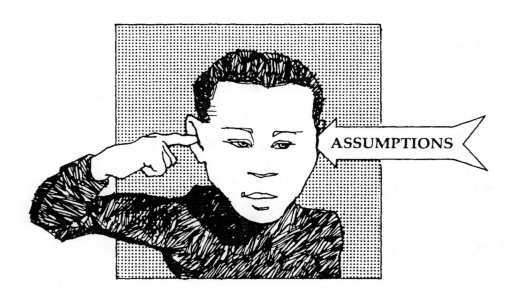

ASSUMPTIONS

BLOCKBUSTER #5

CHECKING ASSUMPTIONS

To avoid solving the wrong problem, while also opening your creative thinking to possible solutions, it is wise to check your assumptions. Begin by asking yourself questions like:

"What are the most likely possibilities?"

"What am I taking for granted?"

"What are some other possible explanations?"

For example, you are at a library and you see a woman put two books in her bag and begin to walk out. What are some possible assumptions?

She is stealing the books.

She is the librarian.

They are her books.

What else?

_____

_____

_____

What could you do to find out if one of the possible assumptions is accurate? (Write your response in the space provided below.)

_____

_____

_____

CONTINUED

CONTINUED

Based on each assumption from the exercise on the previous page what would a possible solution be? (Notice that each assumption leads to a different variety of solutions.)

_____

_____

_____

Can you think of anything at work where your assumptions might be leading you to solve the wrong problem?

_____

_____

_____

How can you check your assumptions for accuracy?

_____

_____

_____

It Always Makes Sense to Check Your Assumptions!

MAKING ASSUMPTIONS—A PUZZLE NINE-DOT PUZZLE

Instructions

Draw four straight lines that go through all nine dots without taking your pen or pencil off the paper. If you have trouble with this, check your assumptions about the rules. Can you find the solutions? If you are really creative, the nine-dot puzzle can be solved with three straight lines. Good luck!

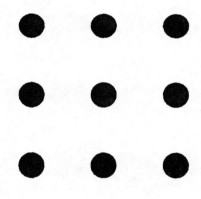

The solution for the nine-dot puzzle is given on the next page.

MAKING ASSUMPTIONS—SOLUTIONS

To solve the puzzle with four straight lines, you must challenge your assumptions that the "rules" meant for you to stay within the dots.

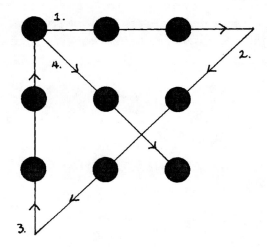

To solve the puzzle with three straight lines, you don't have to go through the center of each dot! (At least the rules do not specify.)

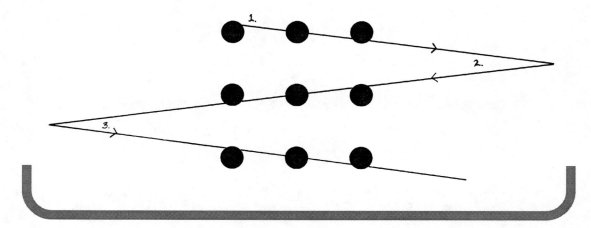

Block #6

Over-Reliance on Logic

Dr. Jonas Salk, developer of the Salk vaccine, said, "When I became a scientist, I would picture myself as a virus or cancer cell and try to imagine what it would be like to be either."

Highly creative thinkers see the advantage of going beyond logical problem solving techniques to include imagination, intuition, emotion, and/or humor.

BLOCKBUSTER #6

YOUR "INTERNAL" CREATIVE CLIMATE

➤ Write out one problem that you have been trying to solve using a purely logical approach.

➤ Stay open-minded and keep a positive mental attitude, close your eyes and let your body relax. State the problem clearly to yourself.

➤ Turn the situation over to your imagination, your intuition, your feelings, and your sense of humor. Play with possibilities, insights, and absurdities. Don't judge your thoughts, just let them come.

➤ Write out key words or thoughts until you feel yourself "pushing" for additional ideas.

➤ Flesh out your ideas by writing for five or ten minutes—allow one thought to lead another.

➤ Retrace your steps to "play with" and discover additional aspects.

Block #7

Believing You Are Not Creative

90% of the knowledge about the human brain and creativity has been discovered in the past 10 years. Research at UCLA's Brain Research Institute indicates that the creative capacity of the human brain is potentially limitless. The only restrictions are self-imposed through our belief systems.

The largest obstacle you may ever have to face is an absolute acceptance of what you believe is or is not possible for you to accomplish.

If You Believe You Can or If You Believe You Can't...You're Right!

BLOCKBUSTER #7

CREATIVE BELIEFS

The human brain is often compared to a computer; using this comparison, it is easy to see that creative results require creative programming! List five beliefs about yourself that would help you grow into a more creative person.

1. _____
2. _____
3. _____
4. _____
5. _____

Some beliefs stand in the way of your creativity. These are the "garbage" in the acronym GIGO (garbage in, garbage out). List five examples of your inhibiting beliefs here.

1. _____
2. _____
3. _____
4. _____
5. _____

When you have completed this list, take a black marker and cross off each idea on the list. Whenever one of the limiting beliefs you wrote down comes into your thoughts, remember you chose to eliminate it. Replace it with a more productive belief that you have decided to retain. For additional reinforcement, write each productive replacement below.

➢ _____
➢ _____
➢ _____
➢ _____
➢ _____

What are you waiting for?

In my seminars, I ask people to evaluate the ways in which they block their own creativity. Over the years I've asked thousands of people, "Why aren't you using your creativity to the fullest? What are you waiting for?" Below are some participants' responses:

Example: "For me to be more creative, I am waiting for... "

> ➤ **The boss to retire.**

> ➤ **The coffee to be ready.**

> ➤ **My kids to be thoughtful, obedient, kind, and self-supporting.**

> ➤ **A winning lottery ticket.**

> ➤ **My turn.**

> ➤ **Someone to bring doughnuts.**

> ➤ **A significant relationship to**
> **(a) begin,**
> **(b) end,**
> **(c) improve.**

> ➤ **A sharp pencil.**

> ➤ **Someone to ask me.**

What about you? What are your waiting for?

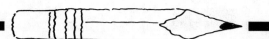

20 WAYS TO DEVELOP YOUR CREATIVE POTENTIAL

Check (✔) those you intend to use within the next month.

I plan to:

❑ 1. Ask "what if" questions—the crazier the better. (What if we all wore bathing suits to work? What if we got paid every day? What if I had to run this organization one day a week?)

❑ 2. Daydream. Let your mind wander.

❑ 3. Write a list of the activities you most enjoy. Vow to spend more time doing some of the things on that list.

❑ 4. Ignite your passion by writing five sentences that begin with "I wish..."

❑ 5. Ask and answer the question, "If we hadn't always done it this way, would we start to do it this way now?"

❑ 6. Write creative affirmations such as "I have faith in my creative problem-solving ability" and "The intuition in me already knows the creative solution for this situation" and read them repeatedly.

❑ 7. Symbolize your creative ability. Finish this sentence: When I'm using my creative potential, I am like a _____. (Example: bright flame). Then any time you need a quick reminder of how creative you can be, think of this symbol.

❑ 8. Play with jigsaw, crossword, and "brainteaser" puzzles.

❑ 9. Pay attention to small ideas—that's where big ones start.

❑ 10. Experiment with different ways of expressing your creativity. (Cooking, painting, photography, dancing, writing, playing tennis, inventing, hosting parties, and so on.)

❑ 11. Notice when you do something creative and keep a "Creative Successes" file.

❑ 12. Imagine yourself five years into the future. See yourself having achieved a major goal. Now go back in time and imagine how this achievement came about.

❑ 13. Play strategy games like chess, checkers, backgammon, or bridge.

(CONTINUED)

(CONTINUED)

☐ 14. Learn a foreign language (and force your brain to think in new patterns).

☐ 15. If you're right-handed, try using your left hand to do things. If you're left-handed, switch to your right for a while.

☐ 16. Draw the Manhattan skyline as it will be in the year 2030.

☐ 17. Ignoring all limits of science, logic, resources, and cost, invent five new products you could use.

☐ 18. Read three-quarters of a novel, stop, and write your own ending.

☐ 19. Stand on your head to get the blood really flowing to your brain.

☐ 20. When stuck for a creative solution, visit a shopping mall, the zoo, or a children's playground and see what new insights these visually stimulating surroundings bring to mind.

PAY ATTENTION

Helen Keller remembered talking to a friend who had just returned from a long walk in the woods. When she asked her friend what she had observed, her friend replied, "Nothing in particular."

"I wondered how it was possible," Helen said, "to walk for an hour through the woods and see nothing of note. I who cannot see find hundreds of things: the delicate symmetry of a leaf, the smooth skin of a silver birch, the rough, shaggy bark of a pine. I who am blind can give one hint to those who see: Use your eyes as if tomorrow you will have been stricken blind.

"Hear the music of voices, the song of a bird, the mighty strains of an orchestra as if you would be stricken deaf tomorrow. Touch each object as if tomorrow your tactile sense would fail. Smell the perfume of flowers, taste with relish each morsel, as if tomorrow you could never taste or smell again. Make the most of every sense. Glory in all the facets and pleasures and beauty of which the world reveals to you."

Techniques for Idea Generation

> *The thing is to become a master, and in your old age to acquire the courage to do what children did when they knew nothing."*
>
> **–Henry Miller, author**

36

What Did You Learn in School?

If you were to go into an average classroom of high school seniors and put a large dot on the blackboard, how do you think they'd answer the question, "What is that?"

Would you agree the most likely answer would be "A dot!"?

Now what if you did the same thing in front of a class of kindergarten children? What kinds of answers do you suppose you'd hear?

Somewhere between the beginning and the end of formal education, we have developed ways to find the "right" answer, but lost the creative impetus to go beyond to find other possible right answers.

What Helps or Hinders?

Highly creative thinkers agree that the first step in becoming more innovative is to generate lots of possibilities.

Some habits and behaviors encourage the production of ideas while others stop idea generation completely. Check (✔) all of these actions you are most likely to do.

HINDERS	**HELPS**
Do you most often:	*or:*

HINDERS — *Do you most often:*

❑ Look for lots of possible right answers

❑ Approach problem solving as "serious" business

❑ Avoid making mistakes as much as possible

❑ Push yourself, even when tired, to keep working on the problem

❑ Ask advice only from "experts"

❑ Dismiss your "silly" ideas

❑ Tell your idea only to people who will agree with it or support it

❑ Keep quiet when you don't understand something

❑ Follow the motto "If it ain't broke, don't fix it"

❑ Not have a system to record ideas that come to you

HELPS — *or:*

❑ Look for the right answer

❑ Have fun with problem solving and "play" with ideas

❑ Accept mistakes as a natural byproduct of the creative process

❑ Take deliberate breaks, when you put the problem on the "back burner"

❑ Get input from a variety of sources

❑ Use your sense of humor as a rich source of possibilities

❑ Encourage feedback from a variety of sources

❑ Risk asking "dumb" questions

❑ Continually look to improve all products, services, and systems

❑ Keep an "idea journal" and record all good ideas

Letting Go of Preconceptions

Zen Buddhists call it "beginner's eyes"—the ability to see things without imposing our expertise and preconceptions on a situation. Paul MacCready, the inventor of the Gossamer Condor—the first human-powered plane to fly a mile—exemplifies an example of beginner's eyes in the creative process. That accomplishment earned MacCready $100,000 in prize money and won his plane a place in the Smithsonian Institute next to the Spirit of St. Louis and the Wright Brothers' plane.

"It's important to start with a clean sheet of paper—to have no preconceptions," says MacCready. "To design the Gossamer Condor, you had to pretend you'd never seen an airplane before. You had to figure out what was the lightest weight structure to make a wing that size, then figure how you'd keep it stable and how to propel it. But you didn't have to do any of this in the way anybody had ever made another airplane.

"If you have too much knowledge of what didn't work in the past and what you think can't work, then you don't try as many things. I was lucky. I had a good background in aerodynamics but none in aircraft structure. So it was much easier for me to come up with a very light and very large airplane, which turned out to be a good way to attack this particular problem."

The One-Minute Idea Generator

On a separate piece of paper, list as many uses for a paperclip as you can think of in one minute. Here are some suggestions to keep in mind:

> ➤ **Go for quantity, not quality of ideas.**

> ➤ **Write down every idea. Do not judge or criticize!**

> ➤ **Stay relaxed, playful, even silly.**

> ➤ **Switch your point of view:** *Look at the paperclip as if you were an insect, as if you were lost in the desert, as if you were a designer, and so on.*

> ➤ **Ask yourself "what if?" questions.** *What if the paperclip was straightened out and a hole drilled through the middle? What if a bunch of them were linked together? What if one end was sharpened to a point?*

> *Time yourself for one minute. Ready—set—go.*

How did you do?

- Were you able to keep writing the full minute?

- Did you run out of ideas?

- Do you still have ideas coming?

 This exercise, using various common objects, is an excellent warm-up technique before a brainstorming session.

Idea-Generating Questions

An excellent technique for generating ideas is the use of Idea-Generating Questions. This can serve as a checklist for possibilities. When you use a checklist such as this, start with a particular item and think about ways to expand it.

> ➤ **What else can it be used for (without any changes)?**

> ➤ **What could be used instead? What else is like this?**

> ➤ **How could it be adopted or modified for a new use?**

> ➤ **What if it was larger/thicker/heavier/stronger?**

> ➤ **What if it was smaller/thinner/lighter/shorter?**

> ➤ **How might it be rearranged/reversed?**

> ➤ **What else?**

EXERCISE: OTHER USES FOR AN UMBRELLA

Imagine that the object you're thinking of is an umbrella. Keeping the questions above in mind, answer the following:

1. **What else could it be used for?** *(Possible answer—to dig holes.)* **What else?**

_____

_____

_____

2. **What could be used instead? What else is like this?** *(Possible answer—a newspaper held over your head.)* **What else?**

_____

_____

_____

(CONTINUED)

3. How could it be adapted for a new use? *(Possible answer—add a flashlight to the handle for people who go out on dark, rainy nights.)* **What else?**

_____

_____

_____

4. What if it was larger/thicker/heavier/stronger? *(Possible answer— make it double size to cover two people.)* **What else?**

_____

_____

_____

5. What if it was smaller/thinner/lighter/shorter? *(Possible answer— make it small enough to fold up and fit inside a purse.)* **What else?**

_____

_____

_____

6. How might it be rearranged/reversed? *(Possible answer—turn it upside down and make a birdbath out of it.)* **What else?**

_____

_____

_____

Different Points of View

Creative thinking begins with idea generation. If you are to have the broadest perspective on a situation, at some point you will need to consider different viewpoints from all people who are involved. The skill of deliberately shifting your point of view to accommodate those of others will allow you to create a more complete list of the factors, consequences, and options involved.

For example, if employees of a chemical company were developing a new pesticide to increase crop yields, it would be to their advantage to consider the following points of view:

> **The Farmer:** Interested in cost of product and how it is applied. Encouraged by reports of increased yield. Concerned about possible toxicity to people and animals.

> **The Company:** Wants more information on production costs, the source of the ingredients, the potential market size, and the expected profit margin.

> **The Consumer:** Worried about the effects of the product on health, taste of food, and price to be paid in the market.

> **The Environmentalist:** Concerned about pollution, contamination, and the ecological effects on the food chain.

> **Others:** (add your own)

_____

_____

_____

_____

_____

_____

_____

_____

EXCERCISE: CREATING AN INTRANET

Suppose you are the manager of employee communications and you want to create an organizational intranet so that employees can access crucial company information. Employees in the organization have never used an intranet and there are several key departments that will have to be responsible for creating and maintaining information on the site. What do you suppose would be the different points of view when you announce your plan? List possible points of view for each.

➤**Your Boss:**_____

_____

_____

➤ **Senior Leadership:** _____

_____

_____

➤ **Front-Line Employees:** _____

_____

_____

➤ **Other Departments in the Organization:** _____

_____

_____

➤ **Are there other points of view you should consider?**

_____

_____

_____

Split Brain Theory

In 1981, Roger Sperry was awarded the Nobel Prize for his proof of the split brain theory. According to Dr. Sperry, the brain has two hemispheres with different, but overlapping, functions. The right and left hemispheres of the brain each specialize in distinct types of thinking processes.

In general, in 95% of all right-handed people, the left side of the brain not only cross-controls the right side of the body, but is also responsible for analytical, linear, verbal, and rational thought. (In most left-handed people, the hemispheric functions are reversed.) It is a left-brain function you rely on when balancing your checkbook, remembering names and dates, or setting goals and objectives. Since most of our concepts of thinking come from Greek logic, left-brained processes are most rewarded in our education system.

The right hemisphere controls the left side of the body and is holistic, imaginative, nonverbal, and artistic. Whenever you recall someone's face, become engrossed in a symphony, or simply daydream, you are engaging in right-brain function. Right-brain processes are less often rewarded in school.

LEFT HEMISPHERE	**RIGHT HEMISPHERE**
Logic	*Intuition*
Sequential	*Non-verbal/Visual*
Verbal	*Spacial*
Linear	*Creative*
Analytical	*Holistic*
Rational	*Artistic*
Explicit	*Humorous/Playful*

Balancing Your Brain Functions

LEFT BRAIN	RIGHT BRAIN
Math	Imagination
Language	Color
Analysis	Rhythm
Writing	Music

Professor Robert Ornstein, of the University of California, found that people who are trained to use one side of their brain "exclusively" were relatively unable to use the other side—even when those functions were needed. When the "weaker" side was stimulated and encouraged to work in cooperation with the other, there was a great increase in overall effectiveness.

How balanced is your workday? (The usual answer is about 70% left-brain and 30% right-brain.)

Here are two simple activities for balancing brain function:

1 **Walking:** According to the co-director of the Walking Center in New York, there is a very dynamic action involving both sides of the brain when walking—and you tend to become more creative.

2 **Breathing:** Research has shown that you can trigger the non-dominant side of your brain by closing off the dominant side of your nose and breathing through your non-dominant side for up to five minutes. (When in need of a right-brain infusion, try pressing your right nostril shut and breathing through your left nostril.)

Whole-Brain Problem Solving

Creative problem solvers understand that both hemispheres of the brain (both thinking processes) are valuable. The trick lies in knowing which function best supports a particular phase of the problem solving process.

Left: Logically defines the problem.

Right: Generates creative possibilities and alternative solutions.

Left: Pragmatically evaluates ideas to determine which are applicable.

Right: Persuades others by sharing your vision and commitment.

Left: Prepares a strategic plan for gaining support and implementing the solution.

In the idea generation phase, right-brain functions become most helpful. Have you ever struggled to solve a problem and found the answer "popped" into your head while you showered or jogged or upon waking? That is because it was released from left-brain control and turned over to your right-brain insight.

> ➤ **The manager of human resources at a manufacturing company in Pittsburgh is most effective generating ideas when she is meditating.**

> ➤ **The vice president of strategic planning at a San Francisco communications company gets his best ideas during his running.**

> ➤ **A marketing representative likes to "sleep on it," telling himself he'll have fresh ideas in the morning.**

> ➤ **A salesperson tells jokes and laughs her way into new insights.**

None of these people are aware they are shifting brain hemisphere functions. All of them simply know (from trial and error) how to get the results they need.

WHERE DO YOU GET YOUR BEST IDEAS?

_____

_____

_____

_____

The Creative Idea Journal

To capture good ideas whenever and wherever they occur, take a pocket-size notebook and write at the top of page 1 this question:

"In what ways might I...?" (fill it in with your own problems). Place the notebook in your purse or pocket. Without focusing on it, let your unconscious mind "incubate" the problem and deliver possible solutions as they "pop up" throughout the day. Enter each idea with the time of day it occurred and the activity you were engaged in at the moment. By the end of the week, you will not only have several usable ideas, you will also know more about your creative "schedule."

IDEA JOURNAL
"IN WHAT WAYS MIGHT I ...."

Intuition

Whether they call it a hunch, a gut feeling, or even ESP (extra-sensory perception), thousands of managers and executives make business deals based on their intuition. Think back over your life. Have you ever had a hunch that you should or should not be doing something? We all have hunches, but many of us ignore or distrust them as being irrational and useless.

➤ **The president of a large restaurant chain headquartered in Vancouver, British Columbia, flabbergasted his employees when he made a command decision to build a restaurant in a rundown warehouse area. Two years later the new restaurant was the chain's top moneymaker and the neighborhood around it was revitalized.**

➤ **The board chairman of a small Australian airline company called his treasurer and told him to spend some money on replacement equipment. Within days, one of the airline's planes unexpectedly needed a costly part.**

➤ **A plant manager of a leading U.S. software company spent most of her time sitting at her desk doing paperwork. But every once in a while she got up from her desk and for reasons not clear to her, walked to a point on the production line and picked out a software diskette that appeared to be okay but proved to be flawed.**

Creative thinkers tend to pay more attention to their feelings, including what they call their "inner voice." Management professor Weston Agor studied hundreds of top managers and found a disproportionate percentage used intuition as an important part of their decision-making process. Most managers first digested all the relevant information and data available, but when the data was conflicting or incomplete, they relied on intuitive approaches to come to a conclusion.

LET ME SLEEP ON IT

Computer whiz Allan Huang had puzzled for months over a recurring dream in which two opposing armies of sorcerers' apprentices carried pails filled with data. Most nights, the two armies marched toward each other, but stopped just short of confrontation. Other times they collided, tying themselves into a big red knot. Then one night, something different happened—the armies marched right into each other, but with no collision. Instead, they passed harmlessly through each other like light passing through light.

Huang had been wrestling for years with the challenge of creating an optical computer. Such a computer would transmit data by means of tiny laser beams passing through prisms, mirrors, and fiber-optic threads. But until the dream opened Huang's eyes to the solution, all the designs he could think of were too cumbersome to build.

Then Huang understood: just like the opposing armies in his last dream, laser beams could pass though one another unchanged. It wasn't necessary to give each laser its own discrete pathway. Armed with his new insight, Huang went on to create the first working optical computer.

BEST TWO OUT OF THREE?

Sigmund Freud came up with a unique way to test out his gut feeling on a problem. He would flip a coin. If the coin said yes and his inclination was to go two out of three, then his intuitive reaction had revealed itself and Freud knew that he was not comfortable with the decision.

EXERCISE: HOW INTUITIVE ARE YOU?

Answer the next 10 questions by indicating your agreement or disagreement with each statement.

1.	I believe in ESP (extra-sensory perception).	YES NO
2.	I have had occasions where I knew exactly what was going to happen beforehand.	YES NO
3.	I trust my instincts when I meet someone for the first time.	YES NO
4.	I often have flashes of insight about an important project.	YES NO
5.	Many of my best decisions were made by "going with my gut feeling."	YES NO
6.	I can often sense a problem before anyone tells me there is one.	YES NO
7.	I have days when I do well because I feel especially lucky.	YES NO
8.	I have had what others would call a psychic experience.	YES NO
9.	Sometimes I am able to dream the answer to a problem.	YES NO
10.	If all the data supported one opinion and my intuition led me strongly to a conflicting decision, I would follow my intuition.	YES NO

Five or more YES scores indicate a high reliance on intuition.
Five or more NO scores show a low reliance on intuition.

Ways to Increase Your Business Intuition

 Practice Foretelling the Future

If you are going to have a business meeting with people you haven't met yet, guess how they'll look, what they'll wear, and how they will approach the business they plan to conduct.

If you're looking for a parking space, anticipate where the first open space will be.

 Imagine Yourself Doing a Task Before the Fact

Not only will you prime your brain for actually doing the task, you will be able to compare your actual performance to the image in your mind.

 Notice Feelings and Inner Sensations You Usually Ignore

Pay attention to internal stirring and feelings. By monitoring them constantly, you are more likely to catch those changes that indicate something has registered unconsciously.

 Keep an Idea Journal

Write down flashes of insight and keep a record of decisions you made on that basis. As you reflect on this "diary" later, you'll be able to evaluate your accuracy.

 Meditate or Learn Self-Hypnosis

Insights are most likely to occur when you first quiet the conscious mind's chatter, then concentrate (focus your attention on one thing), and become receptive to create ideas bubbling up through the subconscious.

 Visualize Symbolically

When faced with a problematic person or situation, create a mental picture that is symbolically representative. (For example, a nurse visualized her confrontations with the hospital's administration as Don Quixote attacking windmills.) Notice any new, creative ideas that come to you as a result of looking at your situation in a unique way.

Exercise: Creative Imagination

This exercise requires at least two people; one to guide the process and one or more others to participate.

Step 1 The participants begin by choosing a specific problem or issue for which they would like additional insights and possibilities.

Step 2 The Guide reads the script (on next page) slowly:

Step 3 Write your clue word on a blank sheet of paper. Immediately write whatever thoughts come to you. Relate this word to your problem-situation. Use free association and write nonstop for at least five minutes.

GUIDE'S SCRIPT

Find a comfortable position, either sitting or lying down. Close your eyes and focus your attention on your breathing. Inhale deeply. (Pause) Exhale fully. (Repeat several times.) With each exhalation think the word RELAX. Allow yourself to begin releasing any physical tension you feel as you imagine a flow of relaxation throughout your body, from the top of your head to the tips of your toes. (Pause for a few seconds.)

Let yourself relax deeply... comfortably... completely. Now as I count from 10 to 1, imagine yourself riding in an elevator... a very special elevator... going deeper with every number I count. (Count slowly.) 10-9-8-7-6-5-4-3-2-1. As you get off the elevator, you enter a very special room. It is your CREATIVITY ROOM, decorated just the way you like it... with furniture, colors, wall decorations, and equipment of your choice. You feel instantly safe and at home here. (Pause for a few seconds.)

Soon you will hear a knock on the door announcing the arrival of your CRE-ATIVITY CONSULTANT. This may be someone you know and have consciously chosen to assist you. Or, your counselor may have been selected subconsciously and you will be surprised when that person appears. In any event, your counselor is symbolic of your creative potential. (Pause.) Now hear the knock and go to the door to greet your consultant. (Pause.) Open the door. (Pause.)

Invite your consultant into the room and explain your problem-situation in full detail. (Pause.) Ask your consultant for any advice or insight. (Pause.) Pay attention if your consultant speaks to you. Be receptive to any idea or feeling that occurs. Notice whatever happens. (Pause.) Ask your consultant for a single word that can help you solve your problem. Listen carefully. (Pause.) If you hear nothing, just clear your mind and let the first word you think of become your clue. Don't be concerned if there is no obvious connection between this word and your problem. Just accept whatever comes to you as having some hidden value. (Pause.)

Now thank your consultant and say good-bye. Look around your room one last time. (Pause.) Think about the word clue that was given to you as you leave your room and enter the elevator. As I count from 1 to 10, feel yourself coming back to this present time and place. (Count slowly.) 1-2-3-4-5-6-7-8-9-10. Open your eyes and say your clue word.

The audiocassette tape of Creative Imagination (exercise recorded by Carol Kinsey Goman) is available from Kinsey Consulting Services, P.O. Box 8255, Berkeley, California, 94707. CGoman@CKG.com.

Phases of Creativity

PHASE 1: *Preparation*

Lay the groundwork. Gather research, background information, specific data, and various opinions. This stage is commonly referred to as "doing your homework."

In the preparation stage, you are searching out any information that might be relevant. Questions to ask yourself include: Have I gathered as many relevant facts and opinions about the situation as I need? Have I explored the possibility that the problem needs to be restated?

PHASE 2: *Immersion*

Become totally absorbed in the problem or situation.

Immersion is the stage in which you immerse yourself in a problem by considering the variety of concerns, angles, opinions, and facts that you have gathered. This is the time to play with various combinations of ideas and stimuli. Let your imagination run free and open your thinking to anything that is vaguely relevant. Allow the unusual and unlikely elements to begin to juxtapose themselves in your thinking.

PHASE 3: *Incubation*

Take time out, a rest period where the total process is turned over to the subconscious mind.

After the rational mind has mulled over all the relevant ingredients and has been pushed to the limit, it is time to surrender the problem and let it simmer in the back of your mind. This is the time when some people "sleep on it," or take a walk, stop for lunch, or work on a completely different project.

The incubation stage of creativity trusts that your subconscious mind will continue to work on the problem and seek a solution when you are consciously monitoring the process. You need to realize that your subconscious is a far more fertile ground for creativity: it has no judgmental or censoring elements, and ideas are free to recombine in unique and novel ways.

Phase 4: *Illumination*

The AHA! experience where insights, possibilities, and answers come; getting that great idea!

With luck, preparation and incubation will lead to illumination; the sudden appearance of the answer (an image, a thought, an insight) breaks through to conscious awareness and comes to you, "as if from nowhere."

Phase 5: *Evaluation*

Test your ideas by taking them through a checklist of criteria for practical applications.

The evaluation phase is the time to get feedback, check assumptions, develop a pilot project, modify and improve your creative idea, and gather support for it.

Questions to ask yourself here are:

> **Have I generated a list of steps and an action plan for putting the idea into use?**

> **Have I chosen the correct criteria for evaluating the effectiveness of this idea?**

> **Have I generated a list of potential supporters?**

Phase 6: *Application*

Put your idea into action. Know that you have confronted and solved the problem by using your creativity.

Translating your creativity into an innovative reality is the final phase. It makes your creative idea more than just a passing thought.

Application means that your idea has become tangible, useful, valuable, and meaningful.

ANOTHER WAY TO LOOK AT IT

Every creative idea goes through three distinct phases:

1. It won't work.

2. It might work but it will cost too much.

3. I knew it was a great idea right from the beginning!

Metaphorical Thinking

Many creative thinkers naturally gravitate to the use of metaphors and analogies in their everyday speech and thought patterns. As a result, their perceptions of situations are normally more colorful and original.

Long accepted as a potent tool for the creative worker, Aristotle wrote that "the greatest thing by far, is to be the master of metaphor." He regarded metaphoric ability (which implies the discernment of linkages between dissimilar objects and conditions) as a mark of genius.

Rules, regulations, and conventions give us order and security. With them we tend to shy away from that which is unknown, strange, or different. One way to expand our creative problem solving is to bypass convention and gain insight through comparison.

EXERCISE: WRITING METAPHORS

1. List as many answers as you can to the question:

    "How is an iceberg like a good idea?"

    Examples: You may have to go a long way to find one.

    Most of it doesn't show.

    What else?

    _____

    _____

    _____

    _____

    _____

    _____

2. Now do the same thing with:

    "How is your job like driving a car on the freeway?"

    Examples: It's a lot easier if everyone follows procedures.

    If you do it in the afternoon, it's hard to stay awake.

    What else?

    _____

    _____

    _____

    _____

    _____

Compare your answers to the author's responses on page 66.

Using Analogies

In science, technology, business, or problem solving in general, it is frequently a metaphor that provides the key to a new invention or theory. Analogies take metaphoric thinking to the next level by creating a comparison between one event or item and something else that has similar elements.

Example: Life is like a grapefruit in that (or because) you just start to enjoy it and it squirts you in the eye.

Life is like reading a good mystery novel in that (or because) the deeper you get into it, the more you wonder how it will turn out.

While creating analogies and using metaphoric thinking, let your imagination and sense of humor go wild.

EXERCISE: IT'S YOUR TURN

Have fun!

Life is like _____ **in that (or because)** _____

_____

Life is like _____ **in that (or because)** _____

_____

Life is like _____ **in that (or because)** _____

_____

Life is like _____ **in that (or because)** _____

_____

Problem-Solving Analogies

A classic example of using an analogy to solve problems is one of a defense contractor that developed a missile that had to fit so closely within its silo it couldn't be pushed in. Using the analogy of a horse that refuses to be pushed into a stall, the solution is to lead it in. The solution for the missile company: pull it in with a cable.

Let's take a look at that process:

Step 1 State Problem *(What is the situation?)*

Missile fits so closely within silo that it can't be pushed in. How then to get it in?

Step 2 Create Analogies *(What else is like this situation?)*

Generate as many possibilities as you can, then choose one to work with. Your list might look like this:

• Trying to get a horse into its stall.

• Trying to get toothpaste back into the tube.

• Trying to get an item back into its shrink-wrap covering.

• Trying to get a car into a too-small garage.

Step 3 Solve the Analogy

To get a horse that can't be pushed into its stall, you need to lead it in.

Step 4 Transfer Solution to Problem

Lead the missile into the silo by pulling it in with a cable.

EXERCISE: PROBLEM SOLVING WITH ANALOGY

Assume that you are the manager of a large department store. Recently increasing losses due to shoplifting have plagued you. How might you reduce shoplifting in your store?

Step 1 **State Problem** *(What is the situation?)*

_____

_____

_____

Step 2 **Create Analogies**

- _____

- _____

- _____

- _____

- _____

Choose your favorite to work with.

Step 3 **Solve the Analogy**

_____

_____

_____

Step 4 **Transfer Solution to Problem**

_____

_____

_____

A possible solution to this problem is outlined on the next page.

AUTHOR'S POSSIBLE SOLUTION USING ANALOGIES

Step 1 State Problem

How do you keep people from shoplifting?

Step 2 Create Analogies

Trying to keep people from shoplifting is like:

1. Trying to keep a cat from eating out of an open can of tuna.

2. Trying to keep kids from sneaking cookies out of the cookie jar.

3. Trying to prevent people from jaywalking

Step 3 Solve the Analogy

Depending on the analogy chosen, a different list of alternatives will become available.

1. How to keep cats from eating out of an open tuna can:
   - cover the can
   - put dog in the same room
   - put tuna in the refrigerator

2. How to keep kids from sneaking cookies from the cookie jar:
   - hide the jar
   - put a lock on the jar
   - give them cookies

3. How to prevent people from jaywalking:
   - erect barriers along the street
   - increase police presence and issue lots of tickets
   - increase awareness through education

(CONTINUED)

AUTHOR'S POSSIBLE SOLUTIONS
(continued)

Step 4 Transfer Solution to Problem

Here are some of the solutions suggested by different analogies:

How to keep people from shoplifting:

- Affix, to merchandise, electronic anti-theft tags that can be removed only by sales staff.

- Cover the display merchandise with clear plastic.

- Put customers in special viewing room.

- Keep merchandise in a case.

- Keep all merchandise, other than a sample, in back room.

- Give away merchandise (as a reward for catching a shoplifter?)

- Have prominently placed video cameras.

- Prosecute all shoplifters.

- Treat shoplifting as an illness.

- Offer support groups and lectures led by reformed shoplifters.

- Develop psychological profile of shoplifters for staff of store.

- Convert store to catalog sales.

- Move the store to another area

AUTHOR RESPONSES FOR WRITING METAPHORS

1. How is an iceberg like a good idea?

- It floats and moves.

- It is slippery.

- It grows bigger and gets anchored at the bottom.

- You will know it when you see it.

- It has a commanding presence.

- It gets a chilly reception.

- It doesn't show the work that has gone into it.

- It is 90% submerged and to appreciate its magnitude, you have to look below the surface.

- It sometimes melts away.

- It can be moved to other places.

- It is difficult to come by.

- It is a wonder of nature.

- When conditions are right, many will be created.

2. How is your job like driving a car on the freeway?

- It is hard to do if you don't keep your eyes open.

- You have to cooperate with other people.

- Some people break the rules.

- It can be noisy and dangerous at times.

- It is confusing until you do it for a while.

- Sometimes you have passengers who nap while you do the work.

- You are in control of the journey. You can pull over, slow down, or accelerate.

- It is challenging and exciting at times and very routine at other times.

- Road signs can help you stay on the right road.

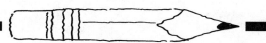

EXERCISE: PERSONAL ANALOGIES

To work with personal analogies, you must creatively project yourself into the situation and identify with a person or thing to the extent that you imagine how it would feel to be this person or object. In this exercise there are no right or wrong answers—just your personal insights.

For example, in the case of the shoplifting problem, you might choose to identify with the shoplifter. If so, you'd begin by asking yourself questions and answering as if you were the thief:

1. **As the shoplifter, what are my thoughts as I walk into the store? What do I see, hear, touch, taste, or smell in the shoplifting situation?**

    Begin with the words, *"As the shoplifter I am motivated to steal something by ..."* and then continue writing using the first person. Let your creative imagination take over.

    _____

    _____

    _____

2. **What are your emotions at the moment of stealing something?**

    _____

    _____

    _____

3. **What different types of noises, lights, or voices might deter you?**

    _____

    _____

    _____

4. **What could happen to cause you to change your mind and not take the goods?**

    _____

    _____

    _____

PERSONAL ANALOGY REVIEW

Go back over the responses you have written and look for insights that could lead to possible solutions.

By using your imagination in this creative way, you can also personify objects. "You are the product" is the role-playing exercise that is especially useful for new-product development. Essentially, participants pretend that they are a new product and talk about how being that product makes them feel, act, or perceive the world.

During a creative problem-solving session, the executives of the Polymer Technology Division of Bausch & Lomb paired off in teams. One person pretended to be an eyeball and the other played Bausch & Lomb's rigid gas-permeable contact lens. The eyeball kept asking for a pillow to cushion the hard and "insensitive" contact lens. The result was a new research effort by Polymer to bond a special space-age cushioning material directly onto the contact lens.

List at least five current situations where you could gain insight by using a personal analogy or playing "you are the product."

1. _____

2. _____

3. _____

4. _____

5. _____

Visual Thinking

Visual aids, in various forms, can be used to boost creativity. Try pinning relevant pictures, notes, or cartoons on a wall you regularly see. The resulting "trigger effect" will help your mind incubate ideas and shape solutions.

One interesting form of visual thinking is called mind mapping. It is simple to do. To begin, take a central theme and write or draw it in the center of a sheet of paper. Circle the main theme and draw lines like spokes whenever new ideas come to mind—writing each idea just above the line that is drawn. If one particular idea suggests another association, draw a branch off that line and write it in.

For instance, if you were the owner of a health spa and were looking for ways to develop your business, your mind map might look like this:

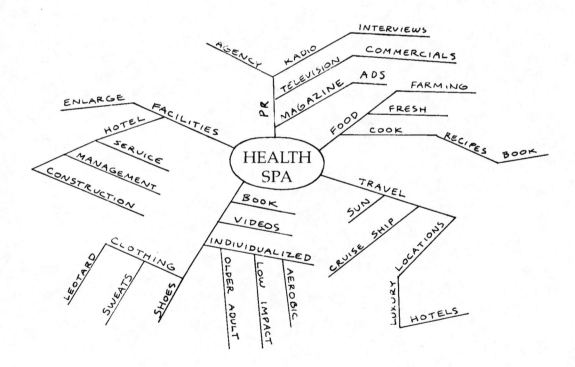

Once you have the knack of letting your mind flow into this visual map, you can use the technique for either business or personal goals. Several corporate executives use mind mapping to prepare informal talks where there has not been time for preparation. One manager used a mind map to decide on the structure and purpose of a project team. As a consultant, the author uses mind mapping to chart annual business goals and posts the map where she will encounter it daily.

70

EXERCISE: CREATE YOUR OWN MIND MAP

Use the space below to experiment with you own mind map. Think about a complex problem in your life and draw a mind map in the space provided below. (Be inventive. Use small drawings or illustrations. Make your spokes different colors.)

Draw your own mind map here.

Group Creativity

"The best way to get good ideas is to have lots of ideas."

–Linus Pauling, Nobel Prize winner, scientist

Managing for Creativity

Are individuals more creative when working separately or as part of a group? What has your experience been? Of course, it will often depend on the personalities involved, but many times we hear of the superior creative efforts of a dedicated group. (The creative teamwork of a world-class advertising agency is one such example.) Why, then, do so many team efforts fall short of the mark? And what can you as a manager or supervisor do to increase the creative output of your work groups?

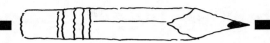

BUILD A CLIMATE FOR CREATIVITY

A manager must be sensitive to the creative needs of employees and design ways to meet these needs while still achieving the goals of the organization. When the following elements are combined, both individual and corporate success is possible. Check (✔) your proficiency below.

	Do Well	Need to Improve
1. Getting to know employees as individuals to learn their creative strengths and needs.	_____	_____
2. Providing training in the basics of creativity to everyone.	_____	_____
3. Guiding and encouraging personal creativity and growth for all.	_____	_____
4. Recognizing and rewarding creative contribution.	_____	_____
5. Ensuring that employees realize that I want and expect creative ideas from everyone.	_____	_____
6. Tolerating failure as an expected part of creativity. Making it safe to take risks.	_____	_____
7. Reducing the stress level through understanding, empathy, and humor.	_____	_____
8. Communicating the mission or vision of the organization and showing how each function supports it.	_____	_____
9. Presenting problem situations as challenging opportunities.	_____	_____
10. Inviting creative participation by all who will be affected by the decision.	_____	_____

This exercise was adapted from Team Building *by Barb Wingfield and Robert Maddux, a Crisp Series book.*

CASE STUDY: CREATIVE DISAGREEMENT

Alfred P. Sloan, CEO of General Motors in the 1920s, revitalized the company at a time when it was close to bankruptcy. At one meeting of his top executives, Sloan said: "Gentlemen, I take it we all are in complete agreement on the decision here." Everyone nodded. "Then I propose we postpone further discussion until our next meeting, to give ourselves time to develop disagreement—and perhaps gain some understanding of what the decision is all about." How proficient are you at encouraging creative disagreement?

Idea Killers

In order to develop creativity in any group, try to eliminate the following responses to a new idea:

- ➤ We tried it before.
- ➤ It would take too much time.
- ➤ It would cost too much.
- ➤ That's not my job.
- ➤ That's not your job.
- ➤ That's not how we do it here.
- ➤ Why don't you put that in writing?
- ➤ It's impossible.
- ➤ Maybe next year.
- ➤ You may be right, but...
- ➤ That's a stupid idea.
- ➤ Our customers would never go for that.

- ➤ You can't do that here.
- ➤ My mind is definitely made up.
- ➤ I don't think that's important.
- ➤ Those people don't count.
- ➤ I don't need any more information.
- ➤ It's good enough.
- ➤ If it ain't broke, don't fix it.
- ➤ Our company is too small.
- ➤ Our company is too big.
- ➤ We don't have time right now.
- ➤ That sounds crazy to me.

Add your own:

_____

_____

_____

_____

_____

Idea Growers

Idea growers are those individuals who elicit contributions by presenting problems as open-ended opportunities for input. They will often say:

- Are there any questions?

- Before we make a final decision, let's review all the options.

- Where else can we go for additional information on that?

- In light of the new information, I've changed my mind.

- May I ask a question?

- Excuse me, I don't think I really understood that.

- Is this what you meant?

- I'd like to get your help with an idea I'm working on.

- How could we improve...?

- What have we missed?

- Who else would be affected?

- What would happen if...?

- Who else has a suggestion?

- Why do we always do it like that?

- Wouldn't it be fun if...?

- I don't know much about that. How about you?

- Let me ask you for some ideas on...

- How many ways could we...?

- What ideas have you come up with?

- Thank you!

Add your own:

_____

_____

_____

_____

_____

Eight Ways to Increase Your Team's Creativity

1 Involve everyone in building creative collaboration. Bring your team together and discuss what it would take to build a more creative and collaborative culture.

2 Ask each member to write down five words that should be added to your team's vocabulary that would help transform the team into one that is more innovative. Combine all the lists and find the top five words.

3 Have your team invent a ceremony that would help establish the importance of creativity and innovation.

4 Have your team write a Creative Vision Statement.

5 Every six months, have members of the team evaluate each other along three simple criteria:

When it comes to team creativity:

I want you to stop doing _____

I want you to continue doing _____

I want you to start doing _____

6 Start a "stolen ideas" contest. Ask team members to submit ideas borrowed from various sources. You might include the following prize categories:

➢ **Best idea from another department.**

➢ **Best ideas from family members.**

➢ **Best idea from a competitor.**

➢ **Best idea from another country.**

➢ **Best idea from a television show or movie.**

7 Stimulate the creative process with props. Science fiction writer Ray Bradbury wrote in a room filled with everything from toy dinosaurs to a globe, from a bag of marbles to a model of the space shuttle. You, too, can use props to help people get ideas and to stimulate creative connections.

8 Know when to retreat. According to the *Wall Street Journal,* a creativity retreat is an up-and-coming tool used not only by executives, but also by teams of employees who find that getting away from the normal routine of business is just what they need to think more creatively.

The P-P-C Technique

As a manager who wants to increase the creativity of team members, the most important question to ask yourself is: "How do I treat new ideas?" Your management skills may be top-notch. In fact, you may even convince everyone that you really want and expect creative contributions. But unless your actions back up your words, you will get nowhere.

When You Don't Agree With an Idea

It is easy to respond positively to a suggestion or innovation with which you agree. But how do you handle that same enthusiastic contributor who comes up with an idea with which you disagree? Have you ever evaluated the idea so harshly that the person (and anyone else within earshot) was totally demoralized? There is no quicker way to halt creativity from the entire group! On the other hand, you can't accept or endorse every piece of creative input just to protect people's feelings.

Use the P-P-C Technique

Following is a technique that might help. It is called the P-P-C. The P-P-C will provide beneficial feedback in situations where you may have reservations about the proposed idea.

Positive.
The first thing you do is comment favorably on things you like about the idea.

Possibilities.
This is where you itemize possible applications or extensions of the idea.

Concerns.
Express your concerns with the proposal in a way that says in a straightforward manner, "Here are some concerns I have. Could you help me understand how they could be overcome?" By directing the situation back to the person involved, you allow the proposer to develop a response to your concerns by designing a pilot project, building a model, or bringing in other examples of similar situations where there has been successes. This also allows the person to reconsider and withdraw the idea.

It's best not to judge others' innovations too critically. An irate banker once told Thomas Edison to "...get that toy out of my office!" so Edison took his invention—the phonograph—somewhere else.

EXERCISE: IMPROVING CUSTOMER SERVICE

Karen is manager of the women's wear section in a major department store. She has wanted to improve the customer service and has asked for creative suggestions from her sales group. One of them, Judith, proposed the following: "I think we should clear a spot to put in comfortable chairs and a coffee table with newspapers and magazines. Then the companions of our customers could wait while the other tries on clothes. We could serve coffee and maybe even wine."

Karen has some reservations about the suggestion. If she wanted to use the P-P-C technique as her evaluation, what might her comments be?

POSITIVES (Example: *"I like your concern regarding companion comfort."*)

1. _____

2. _____

3. _____

POSSIBILITIES (Example: *"We could have merchandise catalogs for them to read while they wait."*)

1. _____

2. _____

3. _____

CONCERNS (Example: *"I don't know if we can dismantle our display area to get the needed extra room. How do you think it could be handled?"*)

1. _____

2. _____

3. _____

Remember to state these as "I have this concern. How could *you* alleviate this for me?"

EXERCISE: NOTES TO YOURSELF

In which situations at work do you want to remember to use the P-P-C technique?

1. _____

2. _____

3. _____

4. _____

5. _____

Circle one of these situations and do a sample P-P-C right now.

POSITIVES	POSSIBILITIES	CONCERNS

Humorous Warm-Ups

Several years ago, some high school students were given a test in creativity. The students were divided into two groups of equal size. The first group enjoyed the half-hour before the test listening to a recording of a comedian. The other group spent the half-hour in silence. The first group did much better than the second group on the creativity test.

Humor and playfulness promote creativity. The next section outlines the procedure for creative brainstorming sessions. But before you proceed, please note: Participation in a humorous activity before a brainstorming session increases creative input. Here are five warm-up exercises to stimulate humorous thinking.

WARM-UP 1: Signs of the Time

Based on the principle of incongruity, this exercise simply moves a common object from one setting to another. Begin by making a list of your favorite signs. Here are a few to get you started:

Now pick a sign and move it to a new location that will make it funny. After you select the location, embellish the image by creating specific details

	EXAMPLE	YOUR TURN
Sign:	ONE WAY	
Normal setting:	*Sign on street*	
New location:	*The boss's office*	
Details:	*Boss is sitting at desk with poster on wall stating "My way or the highway."*	

WARM-UP 2: What Do You Get When You Cross...?

This exercise takes characteristics from two different items and blends them together in a humorous way.

Start by choosing two items to cross; for example, a canary and a gorilla. Then make a list of characteristics that you associate with each item. (The longer the lists, the easier it will be to complete the exercise.)

CANARY	GORILLA
- Is small	- Is large and strong
- Flies	- Lives in jungle
- Is yellow	- Eats bananas
- Sings	- Grunts and beats on chest

Example: *What do you get when you cross a canary with a gorilla? I don't know what it's called, but when it sings, you'd better listen.*

Humorous Warm-Ups (continued)

WARM-UP 3: As I Always Say...

Proverbs supply excellent raw material for creating a humorous look at life. Start the exercise by compiling a list of proverbs. Then choose one of the proverbs and give it a funny twist by adding, deleting, or changing words.

Proverb	Twisted Proverb
Money Can't Buy Love	Money Can't Buy Love, But It Can Make a Good Down Payment On It
If at First You Don't Succeed, Try, Try Again	If at First You Don't Succeed, Blame Someone Else
Only the Good Die Young	Only the Good Die Young, So Our Boss Will Live Forever
Crime Doesn't Pay	
A Stitch in Times Saves Nine	
Laugh and the World Laughs with You	
Two Heads Are Better Than One	
Out of Sight, Out of Mind	

WARM-UP 4: Exaggerate for Comic Effect

Taking statements to the extreme brings humor into them.

Example: *"I was so nervous, my butterflies were flying in formation."*

"I like bargain hunting so much, I will buy anything that's marked down. Last week I came home with a new suit and an escalator."

Practice with these statements:

I was so _____

My _____ *was so* _____

I like/hate _____ *so much, that* _____

WARM-UP 5: "You know it's going to be a bad day when..."

Turn negative thinking into comic relief by exaggerating the things that can go wrong at work.

Examples: *You know it's going to be a bad day when...*

... you see a local news team waiting for you at your car.

... the health inspector condemns your office coffee maker.

... your horn sticks on the freeway behind 32 Hell's Angels.

... the Gypsy fortune-teller offers to refund your money.

_____

_____

Use your imagination and develop your own humous warm-up exercises. Create captions for cartoons, write funny greeting card messages, make up rap songs, or act out a typical day in your department as if you were in a TV sitcom.

Brainstorming

The most popular group creativity technique is brainstorming. Although it is widely practiced, it is seldom used correctly for optimum benefit. Even if you currently use brainstorming, review these rules to check your technique.

Preparation: Prior to the meeting, give each participant an overview of the subject to be brainstormed: The problem statement, background information, and so on.

Send each participant a set of the brainstorming rules.

Brainstorming Rules: The ideal group size is between 5 and 12 people. Ideally all are familiar with the procedure. A facilitator will lead the group, a recorder will write a record of the ideas expressed (usually on a chalkboard or flip chart for the participants to see and review). A timer will also help keep the group moving. The entire group should participate in the idea-generating process.

Part One

Before working on the problem situation, it is a good idea to begin with a warm-up exercise (like the ones in the previous section) to relax and loosen up the group. When you are ready to "get to work," the facilitator states the problem and invites input.

Facilitators should:

> Keep the atmosphere relaxed, fun, and freewheeling.

> Encourage everyone to participate either with original ideas, or "piggybacking" (adding on to) other people's input.

> Focus initially on quantity, not quality of ideas. Some groups set a numerical goal (for example, 25 or 50 ideas) and try to reach it in the allotted time.

> Urge participants to say anything that occurs them, no matter how wild or "far out" those ideas may seem.

> Allow appropriate time (20 to 30 minutes) for the idea generation phase. If the group has been too conservative during this part of the session, the facilitator might want to use the final five minutes and ask, "What are the wildest, most outrageous ideas we can come up with?" (Remember, you may find a gem of an idea that could be altered to fit reality!)

> Stay alert for nonproductive comments such as, "We tried that last year," "That would cost too much," "I don't think that will work," and so on, and counter with, "This isn't the time for evaluation yet." During the idea-generation phase, no one should be allowed to judge, criticize, or squelch any of the ideas generated.

Break:

Before you begin Part Two of brainstorming, the group should be thanked for their participation to the idea-generation phase. Then the team needs to put closure to Part One and take a break before going on. (Indeed, one creative twist that can be effective is to use two groups for generating ideas and switch lists of possibilities for evaluation.)

Brainstorming (continued)

Part Two

The group should reassemble to evaluate the input. As this happens, be sure that each member is familiar with the criteria essential for the evaluation. For instance, if price, human resources, or timing is important, let everyone know. Look at all ideas and suggestions for the value they might contain, both as originally stated and if altered slightly. See if you can scale down an outrageous idea to one that has practical dimensions.

Follow Up:

Regardless of the results of the session, all team members should be thanked for participating. (A short note may be appropriate.) If ideas were suggested that management decides not to implement, your feedback to the group should be in the form of a P-P-C response. If a solution that came from the session is accepted, the entire group must receive full credit!

Brainwriting

With some groups, especially where there is a reluctance to contribute ideas verbally, another technique called brainwriting can replace brainstorming. With brainwriting, you follow a similar set of rules, but instead of speaking the ideas, participants will write them.

Preparation: Prior to the meeting, give each participant an overview of the subject to be brainwritten: the problem statement, background information, and so on.

Send each participant a set of brainwriting rules.

Brainwriting: This can be used with a group of almost any size, broken down into subgroups of 4 to 6. Each group should be seated around a small table. Provide each member of the group with a sheet of paper divided into four columns. A facilitator then explains the rules and announces the amount of time allocated to the session (usually 20 to 30 minutes).

Brainwriting (continued)

Part One

1. At the top of each participant's paper should be a brief description of the problem or solution.

2. Participants are instructed to write four ideas or comments—one in each column.

3. When everyone has completed the four items, they put the papers face down in the center of the table. Shuffle the papers and each person takes one that was written by another participant.

4. At this point everyone will have a piece of paper with four ideas written by another person in the group. On this paper the participants write four more items, either additional original ideas or ideas "piggybacked" on those on the page. This paper is then returned face down to the center of the table.

5. This process is continued until the participants run out of things to write, no matter how wild or "far out" those ideas may seem.

Break:

Before beginning Part Two of brainwriting, the group(s) should be thanked for their participation in the idea-generation phase.

Part Two

Before the group(s) reassembles to evaluate the input, a recorder should collect and compile lists of the input. Make sure that each member is familiar with the criteria essential for the evaluation. Look at all ideas and suggestions for the value they might contain as originally stated and altered slightly. See if you can scale down an outrageous idea to practical dimensions.

Follow Up:

Just as with brainstorming, team members should be recognized and thanked. Suggestions not accepted should be addressed and suggestions accepted should be credited to the group.

Forced Connections

Forcing a connection between two seemingly unrelated things has developed many products: the clock radio, the wristwatch, and the car stereo to name a few. When participants of a group idea-generating session begin to run out of ideas, a facilitator can ask them to look around the room, take something from the environment, and force a connection.

Example: Imagine you are part of a product development team looking at ways to improve the common bathtub. What are some improvements your group might come up with?

1. <u>Make it bigger.</u>

2. <u>Route the warm water to go through pipes to heat the towel rack.</u>

3. <u>Attach a snack tray for those who like to eat in the tub.</u>

What else?

4. _____

5. _____

6. _____

7. _____

8. _____

9. _____

10. _____

Forced Connections (continued)

When your group runs out of things to say the facilitator should ask participants to look around the room and select three objects.

Do so where you are now. What are they?

1. _____

2. _____

3. _____

What ideas might you get for improving a bathtub from each of these things? (A clock might suggest a timer for the tub, a notepad could bring to mind some sort of waterproof tablet and marker, a chair could suggest an entirely different shape, and so on.)

Additional ideas:

4. _____

5. _____

6. _____

7. _____

8. _____

THE "GET FIRED" TECHNIQUE

A favorite way to end a group problem-solving session is to ask participants to take the last few minutes and contribute ideas that would probably work, but are so outrageous they could get the group fired. (Obviously, the task then becomes to scale-down or tone-down the solution so that the problem is solved without risking any jobs!)

Innovation and Practical Solutions

Imagination is more powerful than knowledge."

–Albert Einstein

96

The Politics of Creativity

You may have the best creative idea in the history of your organization. However, unless you know how to persuade others to support and finance your idea, it may never come to light. The politics of creativity require a strategic plan to gather information, convince key people, build coalitions, and obtain trusted feedback.

EXERCISE: SELLING MY CREATIVE IDEAS

To turn your creative idea into an innovative reality, you must be able to gather the support of key people in your organization. The following test measures how well you are prepared to sell your idea to the decision makers.

T = mostly true   F = mostly false

1. Being power conscious in my organization is unworthy of my creative efforts.   _____

2. It is impossible to figure out what will motivate someone else to support my ideas.   _____

3. The only people to whom I will have to sell my ideas are my superiors.   _____

4. It is generally a good plan to "run my idea" by people in advance of asking for their support.   _____

5. One way to gather support for my project is to ask for input from those I expect will be most affected.   _____

6. Irrelevant issues often defeat a good idea.   _____

7. Unless people are willing to give me total support, it is best to withdraw my request for their help.   _____

8. It is wise to get more support, resources, capital, and so on than I think I'll need.   _____

9. People who "invest" in my idea will hope to get something in return.   _____

10. It is better to persuade people, even if I have the power to order them to support my idea.   _____

(CONTINUED)

11. It is important to convert all my opponents to support my idea. _____

12. It is counter-productive to ask for feedback before my idea has been thoroughly thought out. _____

13. I should be sure to get total credit for any innovative ideas I create. _____

14. When selling an idea, any time is as good as any other. _____

15. People are mostly convinced to back new ideas based on the logical details of a presentation. _____

16. The appraisal of my new idea will probably have nothing to do with power and company politics. _____

17. The more I know about the people to whom I am selling my idea, the better I can tailor my presentation. _____

18. It is important for me to support other people's good ideas. _____

19. Unless my ideas generate a major change, I should expect little or no resistance. _____

20. If I really believe in my idea, I should never alter or "compromise" it. _____

Answers on next page.

ANSWERS TO SELLING MY CREATIVE IDEAS

1. **False** Being aware of the power structure of your organization is imperative to your getting your creative efforts recognized.

2. **False** While it might be difficult, the more you research and can address the needs/concerns of your "audience," the better your chances of success.

3. **False** It may be essential to ultimately sell your ideas to key executives; however, many people at different levels in your organization have the power to help or hinder your efforts.

4. **True**

5. **True**

6. **True**

7. **False** Many people might only be willing (or able) to give limited or conditional support to your project. These supporters can still be useful.

8. **True**

9. **True**

10. **True**

11. **False** You will probably never be able to convert every person who opposes your idea.

12. **False** It can be an opportunity to iron out flaws early if you get advance feedback from those whose opinions you trust.

(CONTINUED)

13. **False** A manager once said: "It is amazing what can be accomplished as long as I don't insist on sole credit for the innovation."

14. **False** Timing the presentation and the selling of your idea is a crucial part of your strategic plan for success.

15. **False** While a solid, logical presentation is important, more people are impressed by the depth of your conviction and enthusiasm.

16. **False** It is just as realistic to state that the appraisal of your new idea will have everything to do with power and company politics.

17. **True**

18. **True**

19. **False** Resistance to new ideas should always be anticipated if there is any change.

20. **False** Most good ideas have been altered to better fit a particular climate or application.

Interpretation

Give yourself two points for every correct answer and zero if it was wrong. Your score represents your overall level of understanding of what it takes to sell your idea.

Low Level	Medium Level	High Level
0 - 10	20	30 - 40

Strengthening Your Presentation

When presenting your new idea, you may bolster your position by citing an outside source. See if you can strengthen your argument by including:

> **Examples from other organizations** (within or outside of your field) that have used a similar idea successfully. If others are doing something similar and it works, your organization may feel safer in trying it.

> **Business and technical journals** that have published articles on ideas similar to yours. Quoting from relevant published materials can add credence to your statements.

> **Consultants who have experience implementing new ideas** in other organizations. Not only can they help plan your strategy, they may also be quoted on their unique perspectives on the implementation process of others.

> **Company publications** in which articles appear on the topic of change, creativity, or innovative contributions. If you can use direct statements from top executives that support your position (and then hand out a copy of the article quoted) you may gain strength.

> **Recent organizational data** including charts, graphs, and so on, that deal directly with your topic and its cost/added-value to the organization. Being prepared and informed will build your creativity.

Basic Considerations in Selling an Idea

Success in launching a new idea or program depends, to a large degree, on how well you have strategized the selling of your idea. The political aspects of your plan require a sensitivity to the power structure in your organization, especially on knowing how your idea addresses the wants or needs of others.

Here are some basic items to consider when developing your strategic plan: Ask yourself these questions early and often!

> ➤ **Can I state the most important features of my idea simply and clearly?** (Don't assume the facts will speak for themselves. Others may draw significantly different conclusions from the facts than you did.)

> ➤ **What are my personal assets and strengths?**

_____

_____

> ➤ **What are my personal weaknesses and liabilities?**

_____

_____

> ➤ **Who will be affected if my idea gets implemented?**

_____

_____

> ➤ **Who are (or can become) my major allies?**

_____

_____

> ➤ **Who will be my opponents?**

_____

_____

Basic Considerations in
Selling an Idea (continued)

➤ **Why will supporters back me?** (How will their interests or concerns be addressed?)

_____

_____

➤ **What are the strengths and weaknesses of my opponents?**

_____

_____

➤ **Where can I anticipate resistance and how can I minimize its impact?**

_____

_____

➤ **Who will I need to add to my coalition of supporters?**

_____

_____

➤ **How can I attract these individuals?**

_____

_____

➤ **Whom can I count on for feedback I can trust?**

_____

_____

➤ **How will the implementation of my idea serve the mission of the organization?**

_____

_____

➤ **What is the competition doing in this area?**

_____

_____

➤ **How could I implement or test this idea in a way that would minimize the risk for others and myself?**

_____

_____

➤ **Why am I so committed to this idea?**

_____

_____

My Personal Assessment and Action Plan

The best intentions in the world lead nowhere unless they are put into action. You already have all the creative potential you will ever need. Now it's up to you to apply that creativity in your daily work. By completing this book you are well on your way to increasing your creativity and innovation on the job.

You have learned many creative techniques. Where will you use them?

➤ **Current applications of *Creativity in Business*** (Where in your work life do you already express your creativity?)

_____

_____

_____

_____

➤ **Areas in business where you could use more creativity** (Where do you feel a need for more creativity and innovation?)

_____

_____

_____

_____

➤ **Creativity resources** (What specific techniques from the book could you use to increase your creativity where it's needed?)

_____

_____

_____

_____

When specifically are you going to put these creativity techniques into action?

Situation #1:_____ Date _____

Creativity Technique: _____

_____

Situation #2:_____ Date _____

Creativity Technique: _____

_____

Situation #3:_____ Date _____

Creativity Technique: _____

_____

Situation #4:_____ Date _____

Creativity Technique: _____

_____

Situation #5:_____ Date _____

Creativity Technique: _____

_____

Situation #6:_____ Date _____

Creativity Technique: _____

_____

NOTES

NOTES

NOTES

Also Available

Books•Videos•Computer-Based Training Products

If you enjoyed this book, we have great news for you. There are over 200 books available in the *Crisp Fifty-Minute™ Series*. For more information visit us online at www.axzopress.com

Subject Areas Include:

Management
Human Resources
Communication Skills
Personal Development
Sales/Marketing
Finance
Coaching and Mentoring
Customer Service/Quality
Small Business and Entrepreneurship
Training
Life Planning
Writing